The Jazz Piano Collection

T0066060

Amsco Publications
part of The Music Sales Group
London / New York / Paris / Sydney / Copenhagen / Berlin / Madrid / Tokyo

This book © Copyright 2008 by Amsco Publications,
a division of Music Sales Corporation.

Unauthorized reproduction of any part
of this publication by any means including
photocopying is an infringement of copyright.

Exclusive distributors:
Music Sales Corporation,
257 Park Avenue South, New York, NY 10010.

Music Sales Limited,
14-15 Berners Street, London, W1T 3LJ, UK.

Music Sales Pty Limited,
20 Resolution Drive,
Caringbah, NSW 2229, Australia.

Order No. AM987305
ISBN 978-0-8256-3581-6

Arranged and engraved by David Pearl.
Cover Design by Ruth Keating.

Printed in the Unites States of America by
Vicks Lithograph and Printing Corporation.

Your Guarantee of Quality:

As publishers, we strive to produce every book
to the highest commercial standards.

The music has been freshly engraved, and the book has been
carefully designed to minimize awkward page turns to make
playing from it a real pleasure. Particular care has been given
to specifying acid-free, neutral-sized paper made from pulps
that have not been elemental chlorine bleached.

This pulp is from farmed sustainable forests and
was produced with special regard for the environment.

Throughout, the printing and binding have been planned to ensure
a sturdy, attractive publication, which should give years of enjoyment.

If your copy fails to meet our high standards, please inform us
and we will gladly replace it.

www.learnasyouplay.com

Anthropology

By Dizzy Gillespie and Charlie Parker

Fast Swing ($\quad$ = 86)

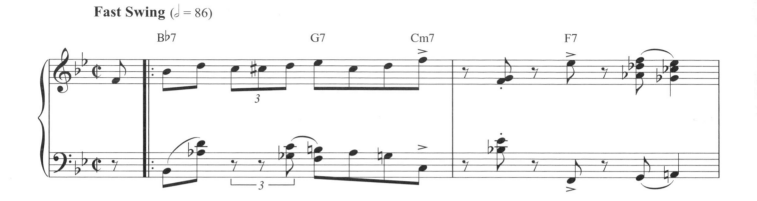

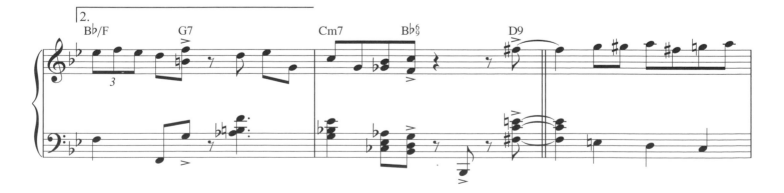

Copyright © 1948 (renewed) by Music Sales Corporation (ASCAP) and Atlantic Music Corporation.
International Copyright Secured. All Rights Reserved. Reprinted by Permission.

Bye Bye Blackbird

By Mort Dixon and Ray Henderson

Copyright © 1951, 1979 (renewed) Olde Clover Leaf Music (ASCAP). Administered by Bug / Ray Henderson Music (ASCAP).

All Rights in the U.S.A. controlled by Olde Clover Leaf Music (ASCAP). Administered by Bug / Ray Henderson Music (ASCAP).

All Rights in Canada controlled by Redwood Music Limited.

All Rights Reserved. Used by Permission.

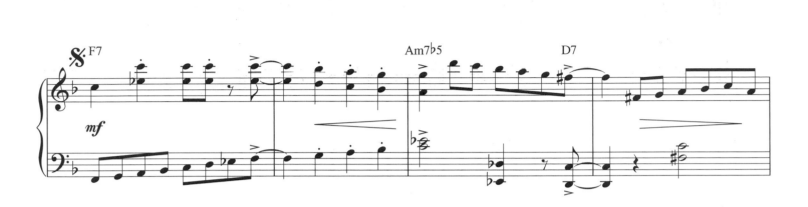

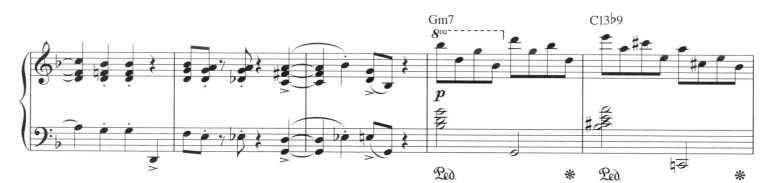

The Girl from Ipanema
(Garota de Ipanema)

Music by Antonio Carlos Jobim
English Words by Norman Gimbel
Original Words by Vinicius de Moraes

Bossa nova (♩=112)

Copyright © 1963 Antonio Carlos Jobim and Vinicius de Moraes. Copyright renewed 1991 and assigned to Songs of Universal, Inc. and New Thunder Music, Inc.
English Words renewed 1991 by Norman Gimbel for the World and assigned to New Thunder Music, Inc. administered by Gimbel Music Group, Inc.
All Rights Reserved. Used by Permission.

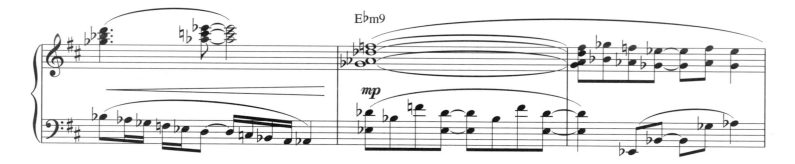

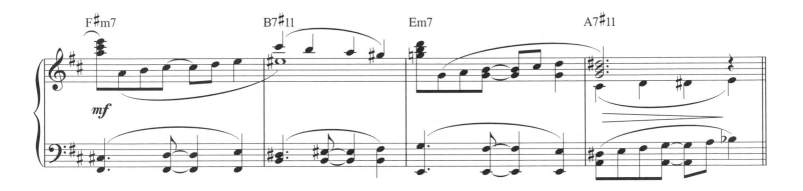

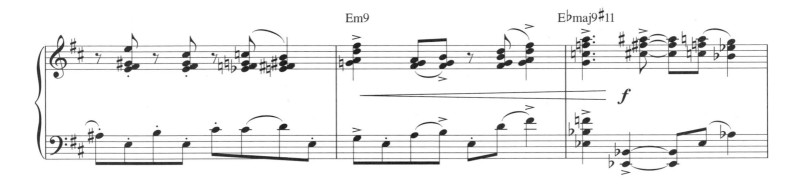

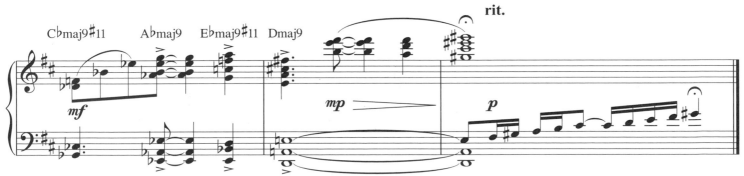

Cherokee
(Indian Love Song)

Words and Music by Ray Noble

Very fast (♩=140)

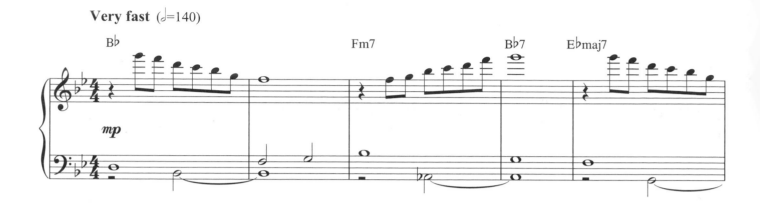

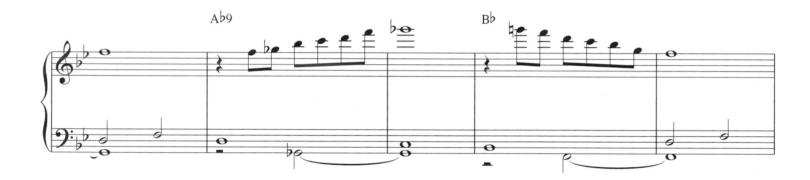

Copyright © 1938 The Peter Maurice Music Co., Limited.
Copyright renewed and assigned to Shapiro, Bernstein & Co., Inc., for U.S.A. and Canada.
International Copyright Secured. All Rights Reserved. Used by Permission.

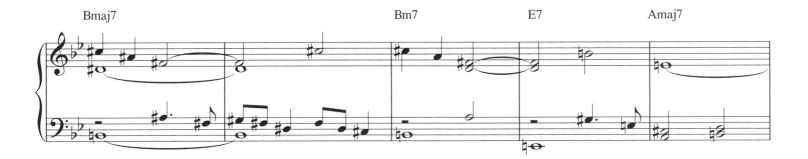

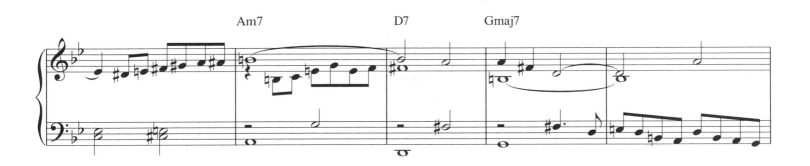

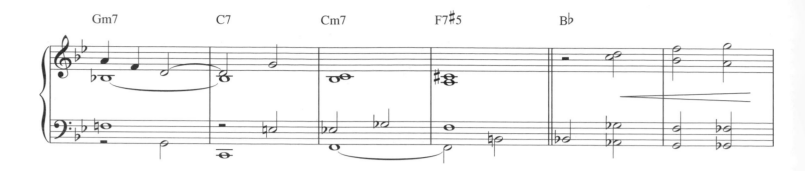

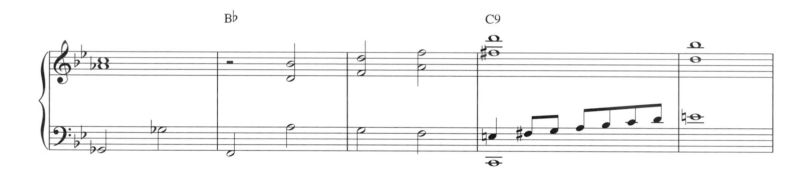

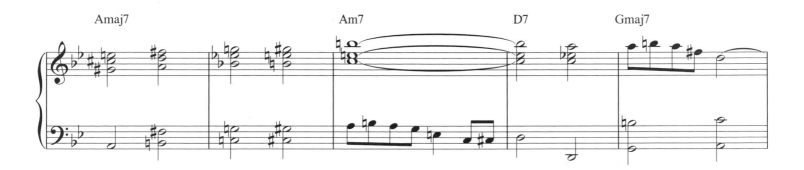

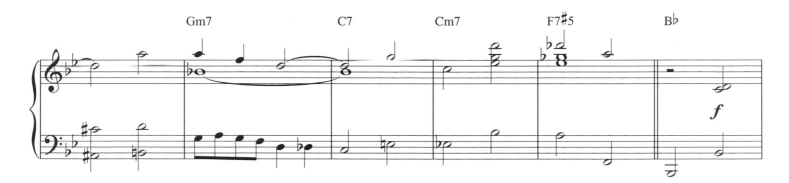

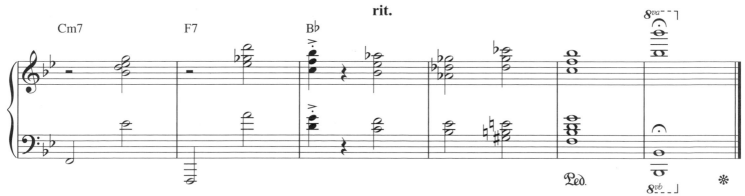

Desafinado
(Slightly Out of Tune)

By Antonio Carlos Jobim and Newton Ferreira Mendonca

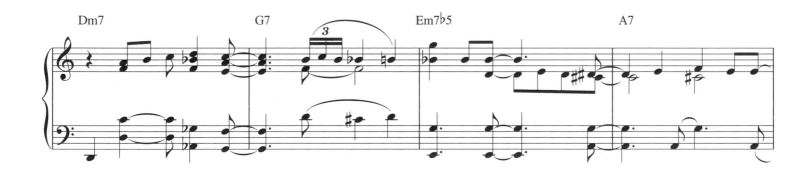

Copyright © 1958, 1962 (renewed) by Editora Arapua / Corcovado Music / Bendig Music Corporation (BMI).
All Rights in the U.S.A. controlled by Editora Arapua / Corcovado Music / Bendig Music Corporation (BMI).
International Copyright Secured. All Rights Reserved. Used by Permission.

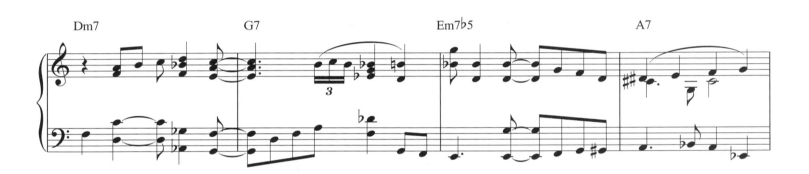

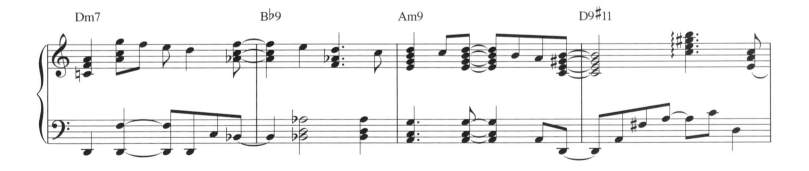

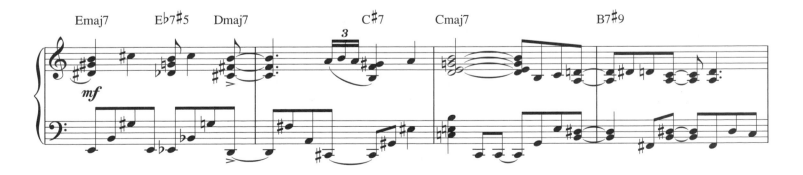

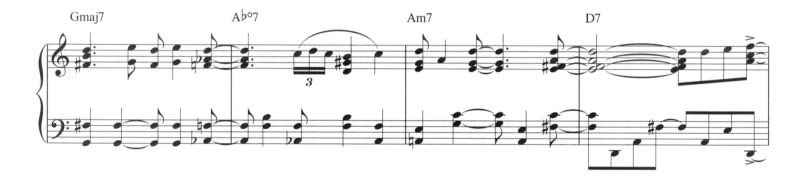

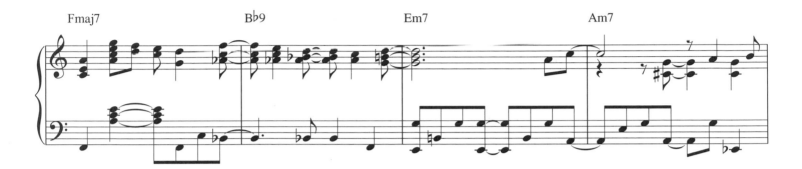

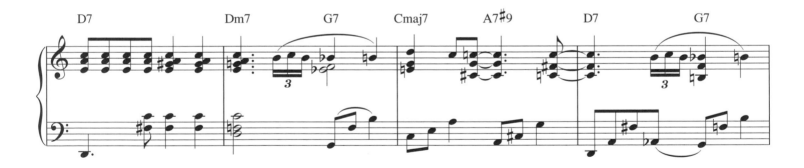

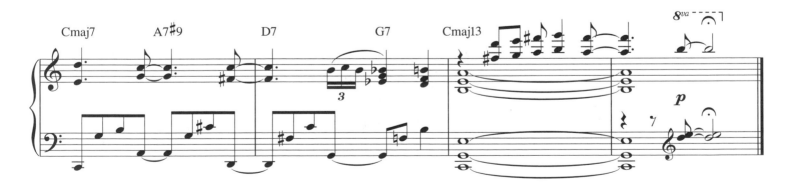

Donna Lee

By Charlie Parker

Fast Swing (♩=180)

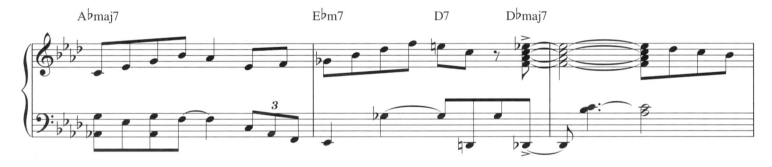

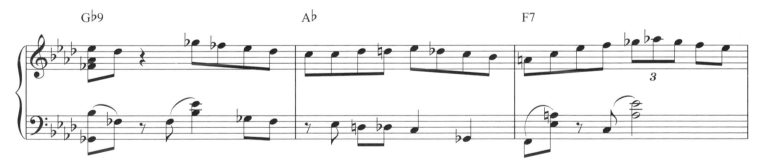

Copyright © 1947 (renewed 1975) Atlantic Music Corporation.
All Rights for the World excluding the U.S.A. controlled and administered by Screen Gems-EMI Music, Inc.
All Rights Reserved. International Copyright Secured. Used by Permission.

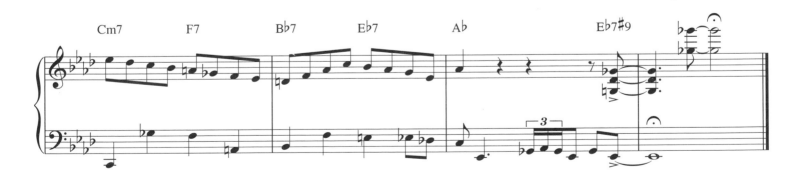

Epistrophy

By Kenneth Clark and Thelonious Monk

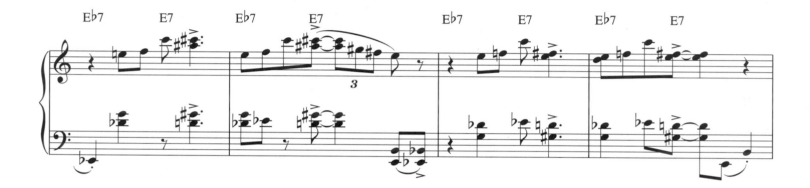

Copyright © 1947 (renewed) by Embassy Music Corporation and Music Sales Corporation.
International Copyright Secured. All Rights Reserved. Used by Permission.

Goodbye Pork Pie Hat

By Charles Mingus

Slow Swing (♩=60)

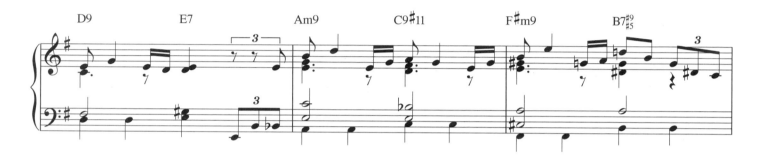

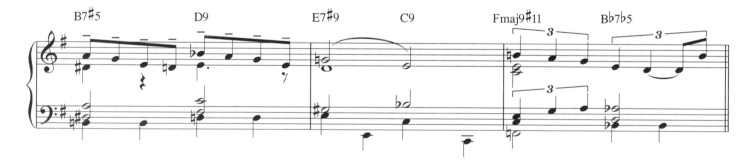

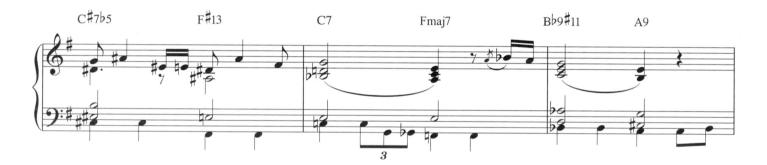

Copyright © 1975 Jazz Workshop, Inc.

All Rights Reserved. Used by Permission.

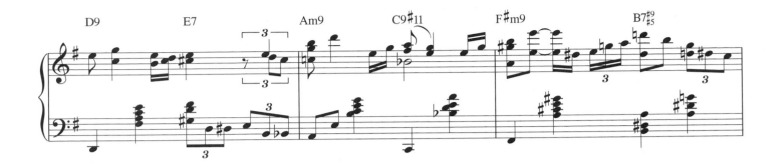

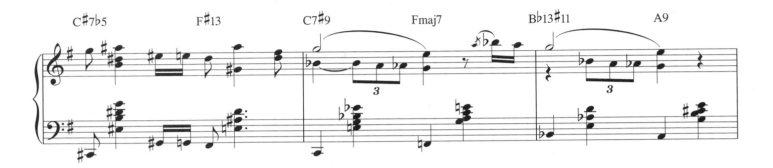

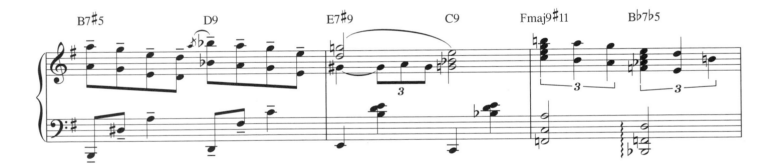

Freely

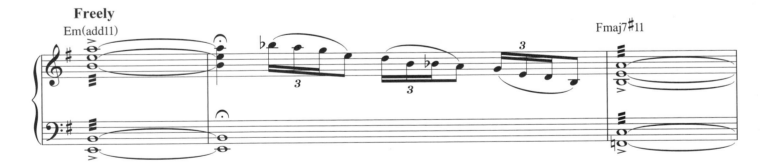

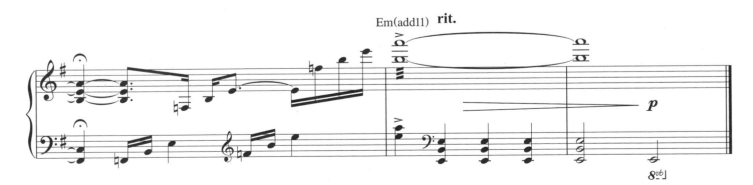

Lady Bird

By Tadd Dameron

Moderate Swing (♩=112)

Copyright © 1947 (renewed) by Music Sales Corporation (ASCAP).
International Copyright Secured. All Rights Reserved. Reprinted by Permission.

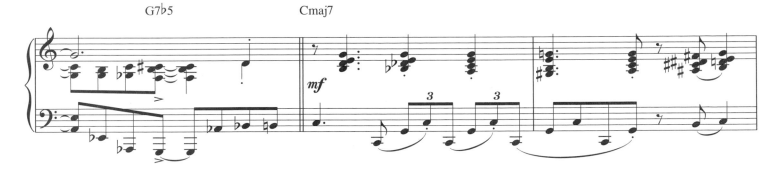

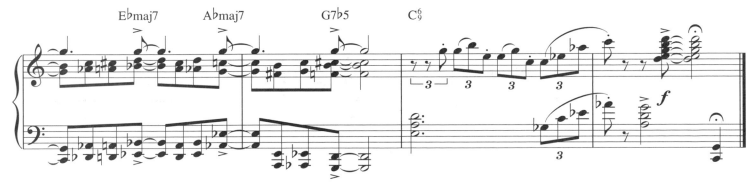

Lullaby of Birdland

Words by George David Weiss
Music by George Shearing

Moderate swing (♩=104)

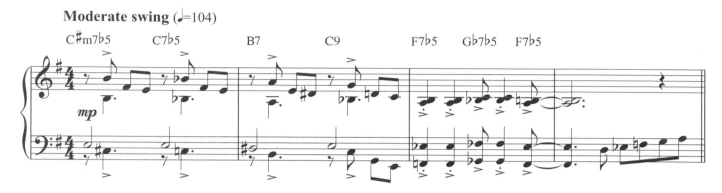

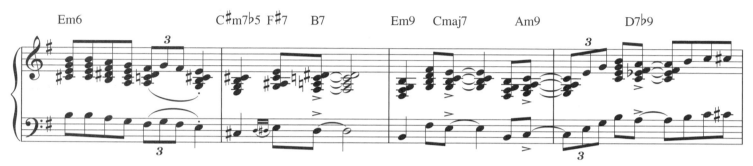

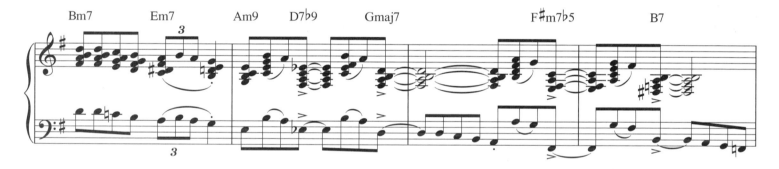

Copyright © 1952, 1954 (renewed 1980, 1982) EMI Longitude Music.

All Rights Reserved. International Copyright Secured. Used by Permission.

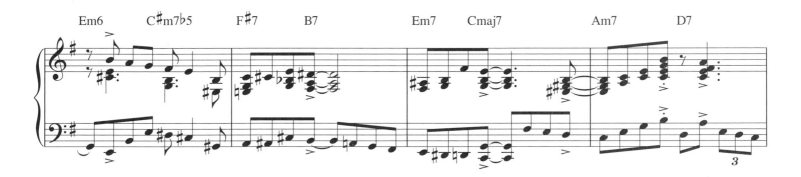

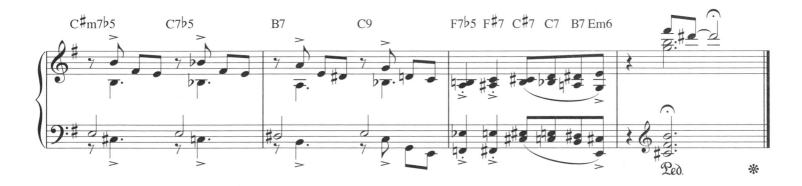

Lush Life

Words and Music by Billy Strayhorn

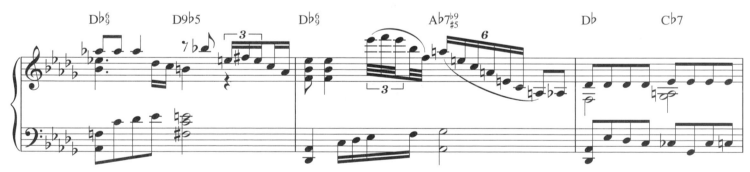

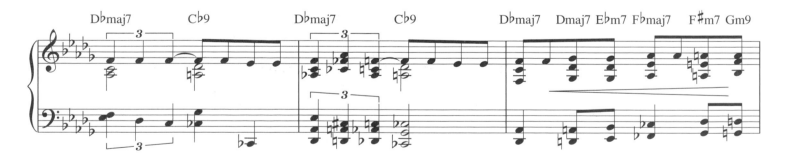

Copyright © 1949 (renewed) Music of 1091 (ASCAP) and Billy Strayhorn Songs (ASCAP).
All Rights in the U.S.A. administered by Cherry Lane Publishing Company, Inc.
All Rights outside of U.S.A. controlled by Music Sales Corporation (ASCAP) and Tempo Music, Inc. (ASCAP). All Rights administered by Music Sales Corporation.
International Copyright Secured. All Rights Reserved.

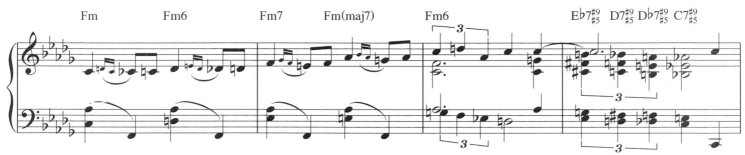

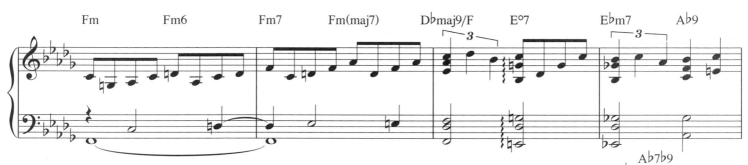

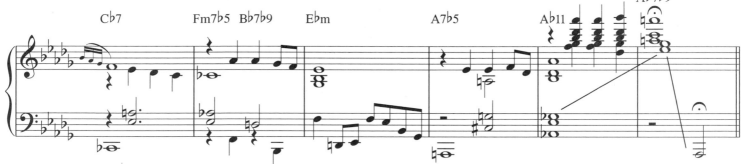

Mercy, Mercy, Mercy

By Josef Zawinul

Moderate Rock (♩=96)

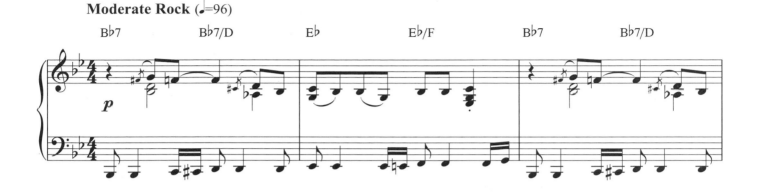

Copyright © 1966 (renewed) by Zawinul Music, a division of Gopam Enterprises, Inc.

All Rights Reserved. Used by Permission.

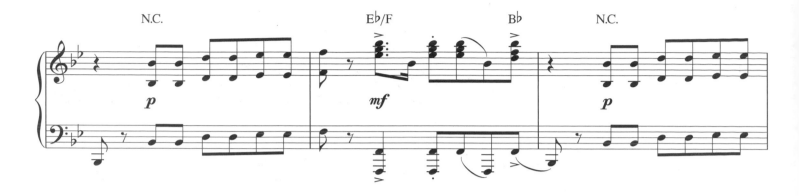

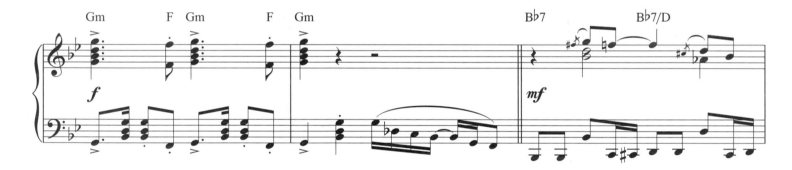

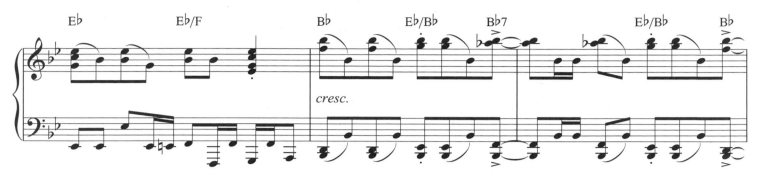

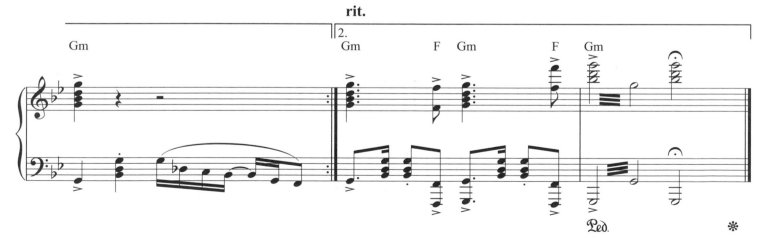

Manteca

By Dizzy Gillespie, Gil Walter Fuller & Luciano Gonzales

Copyright © 1948 (renewed) by Music Sales Corporation (ASCAP) and Twenty Eighth Street Music.
International Copyright Secured. All Rights Reserved. Reprinted by Permission.

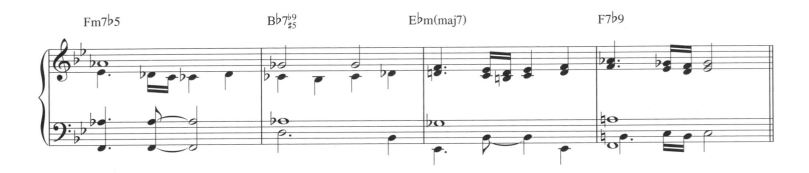

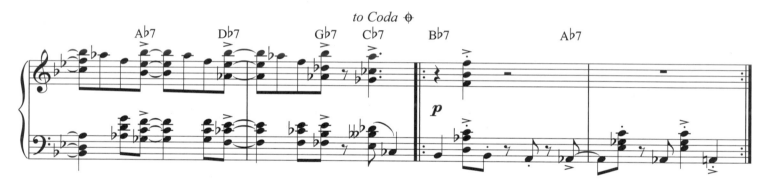

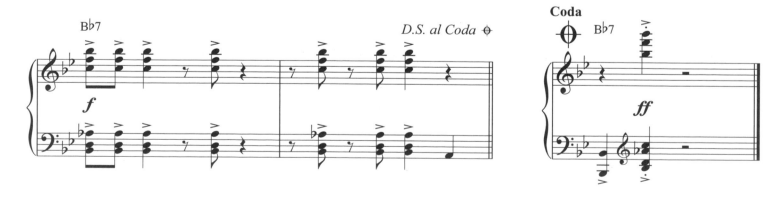

Poinciana

Words and Music by Nat Simon and Buddy Bernier

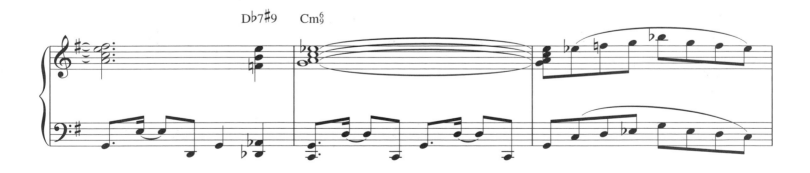

Copyright © 1936 (renewed) Chappell & Co. / Bernier Publishing.

All Rights Reserved. Used by Permission.

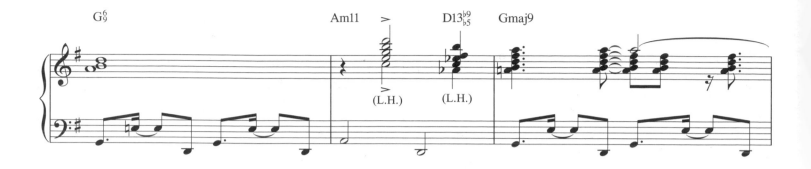

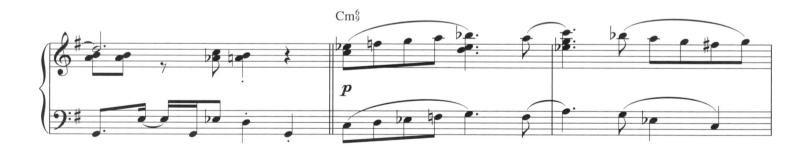

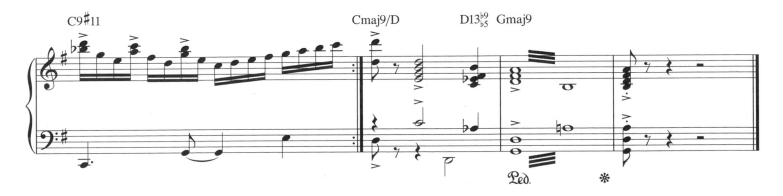

Now's the Time

By Charlie Parker

Moderate Swing (♩=126)

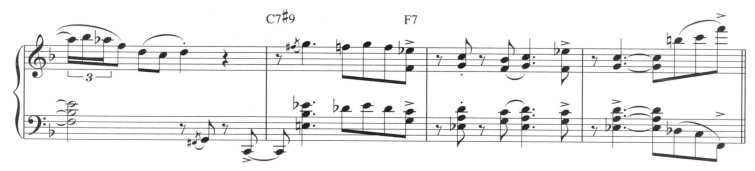

Copyright © 1945 (renewed 1973) Atlantic Music Corporation. All Rights for the World excluding the U.S.A. controlled and administered by Screen Gems-EMI Music, Inc.
All Rights Reserved. International Copyright Secured. Used by Permission.

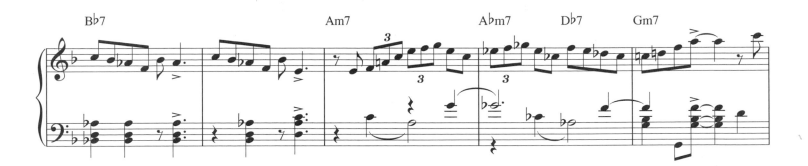

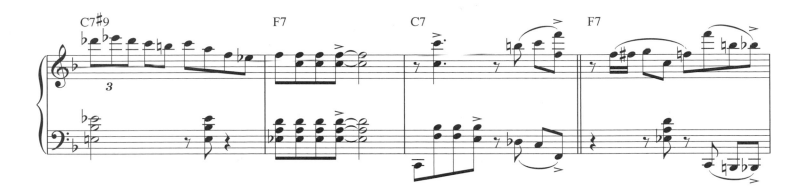

Perdido

By Ervin Drake, Harry Lenk & Juan Tizol

Fast Swing (♩=168)

Copyright © 1942, 1944 (renewed) by Music Sales Corporation (ASCAP) and Tempo Music, Inc.
All Rights Administered by Music Sales Corporation (ASCAP).
International Copyright Secured. All Rights Reserved. Reprinted by Permission.

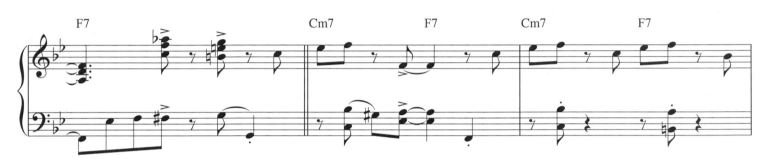

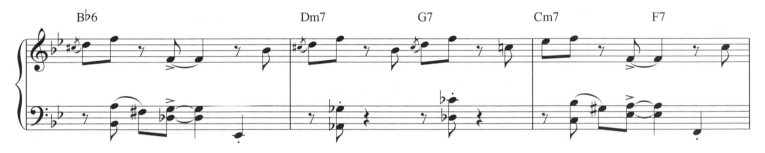

Ruby, My Dear

Words and Music by Thelonious Monk

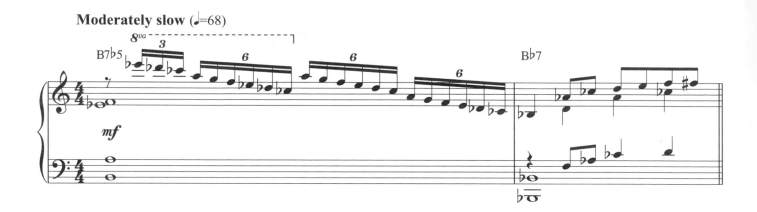

Copyright © 1945 (renewed) by Embassy Music Corporation (BMI). All Rights outside the U.S.A. controlled by Music Sales Corporation (ASCAP).
International Copyright Secured. All Rights Reserved. Reprinted by Permission.

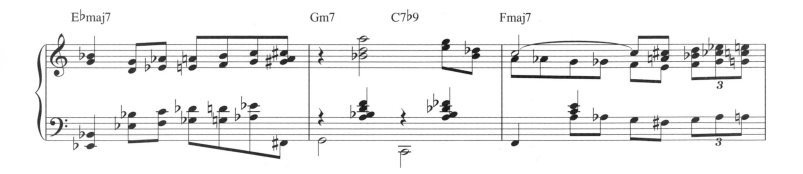

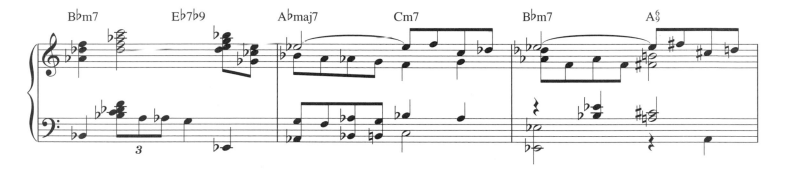

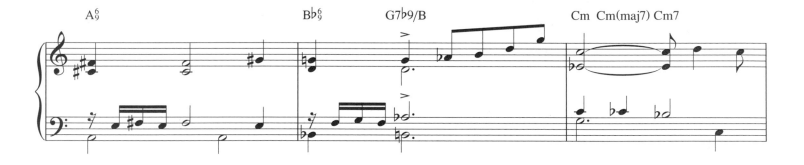

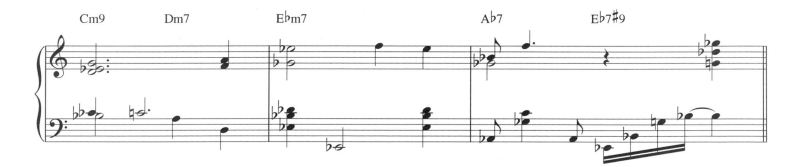

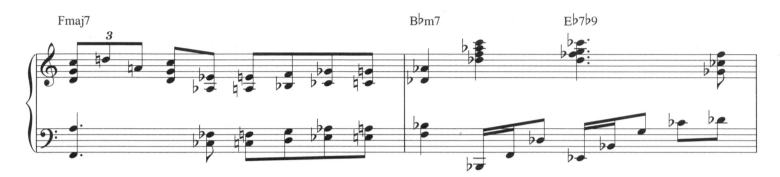

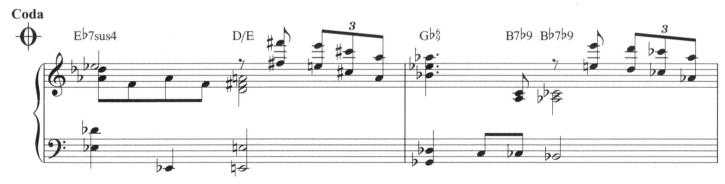

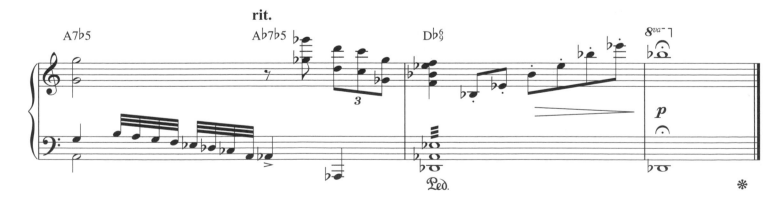

Spain

By Chick Corea

Fast, in 2 ($\quarternote$=120)

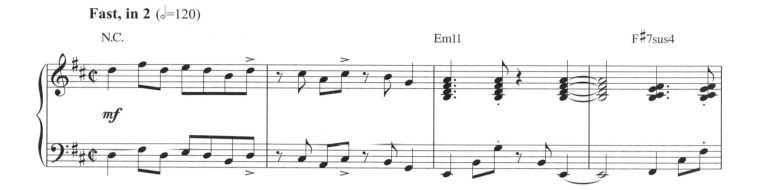

Copyright © 1973, 1982 (renewed) Universal Music Corporation.

All Rights Reserved. Used by Permission.

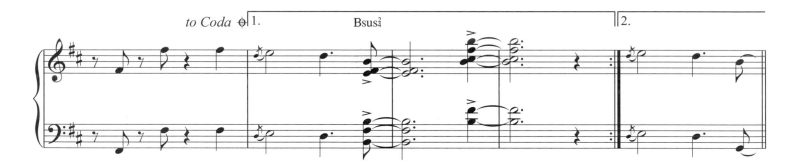

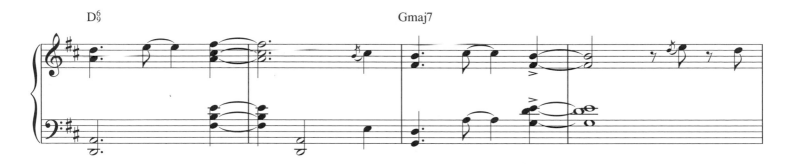

Coda

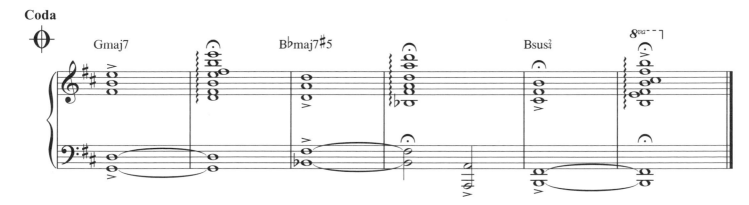

51

St. Thomas

By Sonny Rollins

Fast, in 2 (♩=100)

Copyright © 1963 (renewed) Prestige Music.
International Copyright Secured. All Rights Reserved.

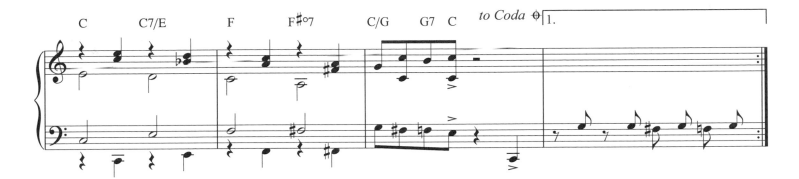

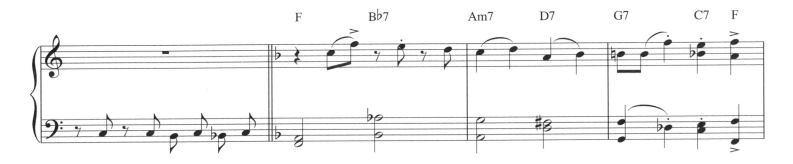

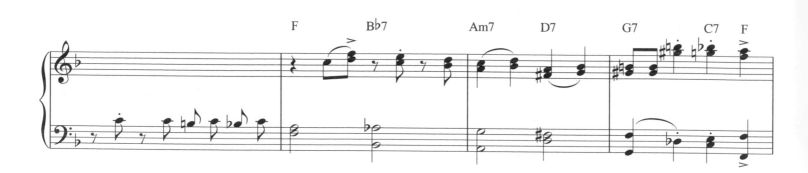

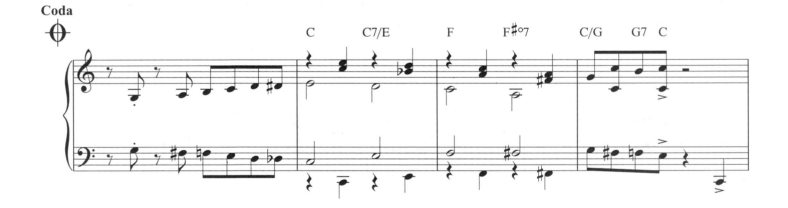

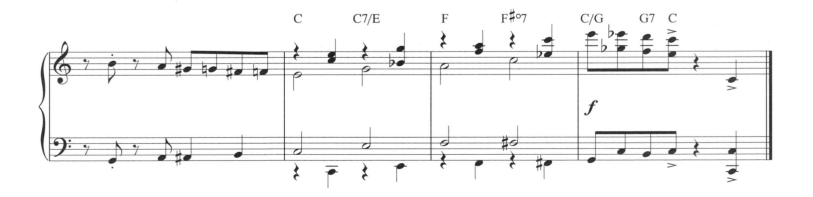

Scrapple from the Apple

By Charlie Parker

Moderately fast Swing (♩=148)

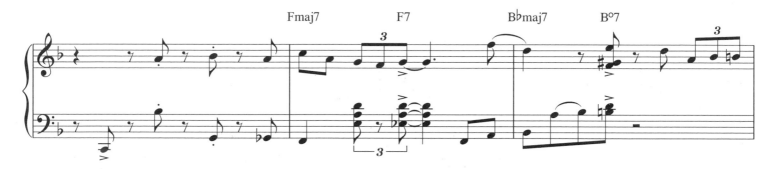

Copyright © 1957–1985 Atlantic Music Corporation.
All Rights Reserved. International Copyright Secured. Used by Permission.

So What

By Miles Davis

Moderate Swing (♩=126)

Copyright © 1959 (renewed) Jazz Horn Music.
All Rights administered by Sony/ATV Music Publishing.
International Copyright Secured. All Rights Reserved.

Dm7

to Coda ⊕

N.C.

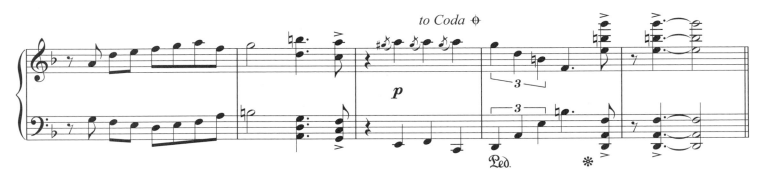

1.   2.   *D.S. al Coda* ⊕

⊕ **Coda**

Waltz for Debby

Music by Bill Evans
Lyrics by Gene Lees

Moderately fast (♩ = 160)

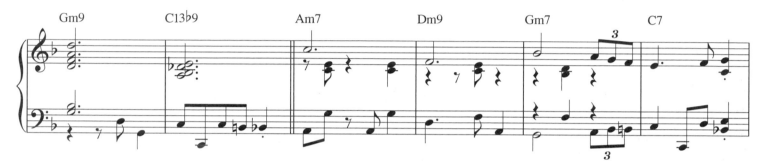

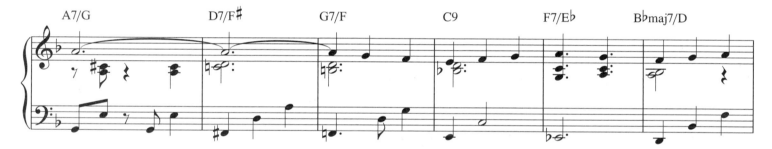

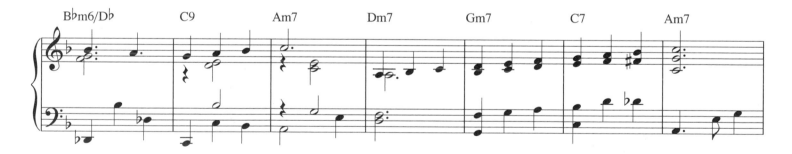

Copyright © 1964 (renewed), 1965 (renewed), 1966 (renewed) Folkways Music Publishers, Inc.
International Copyright Secured. All Rights Reserved.

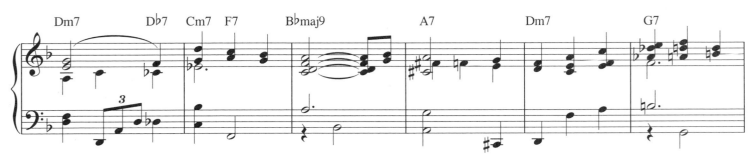

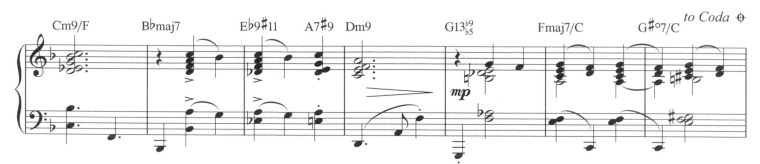

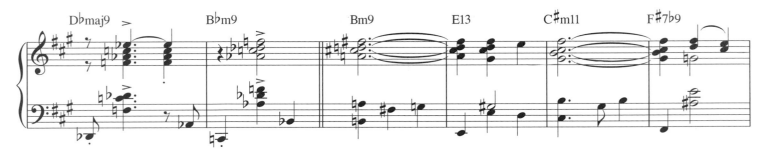

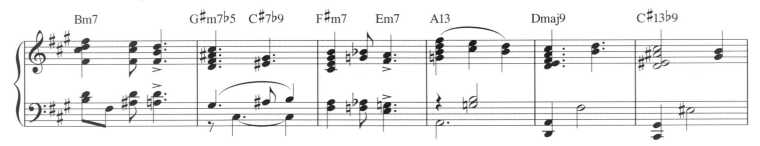

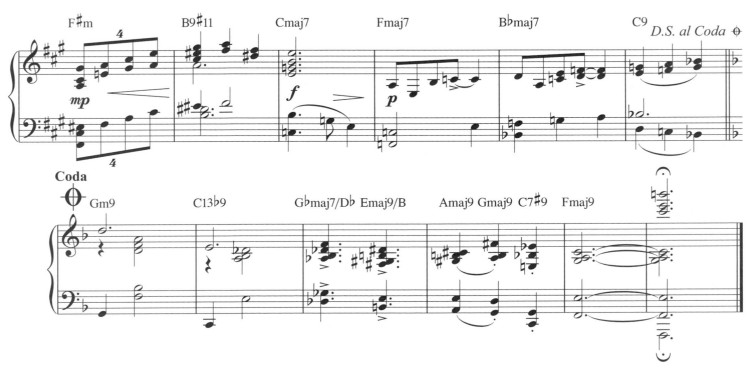